"May this book help you to connect to the Blessing of the Lord. And may the Lord make you an evidence of His Blessing in your generation, in the Name of Jesus Christ. Amen!"

This book is a gift from:..

To:..

Date:..

BEST SELLER

Purpose, Products, and Pathways to

The
Blessing

Experiencing the Substantiality,
Materiality, and Tangibility of God's Blessing

The Blessing of God is the curse-proof, trouble-proof, and struggle-proof dressing of God on a man. It is the goodwill backing or pronouncement of God over a person's life.

Paul Enenche

PURPOSE, PRODUCTS, & PATHWAYS TO

THE BLESSING

Experiencing the Substantiality, Materiality and Tangibility of God's Blessing

PAUL ENENCHE MD

PURPOSE, PRODUCTS, & PATHWAYS TO THE BLESSING

" Your Blessings
Lord, are irreverssible
No Curse on Earth can
Undo Your Blessing...
"

I'm Blessed!

Song Received and Written
by Dr. (Pst.) Paul Enenche

Your promises Lord are Yea and Amen.
Your mercy endureth forevermore
Oh and Your Blessing Lord is a dressing of peace
And it maketh rich and addeth no sorrow

Chorus
I'm blessed with the blessings of Abraham
I'm blessed with the restfulness of Isaac
And I'm blessed with the limitlessness of Jacob
For Christ redeemed me from the curse of the Law

Your Blessings Lord are irreversible
No curse on earth can undo Your Blessing
Whom You have Blessed on earth
O Lord, is blessed indeed
For Your power is at the back of Your Word

Your Blessing Lord is a preservative
No force on earth can destroy the blessed one
For whom You blessed You also defend by Your Might
For Your Blessing is Your investment in men

Dr. (Pst.) Paul &
Dr. (Mrs) Becky Enenche

"

God knows the content of your character
and the destination of your future. He
knows who has the capacity and stamina to
take you where He wants you to go...When
you come under the right spiritual authority,
the Blessing is a natural outflow. You don't
struggle for it.

"

Step into the Next Level of Life!

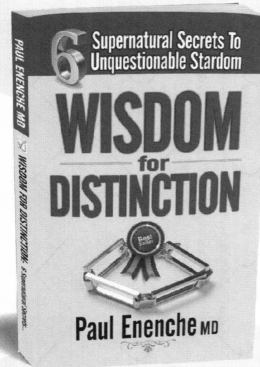

6 Supernatural Secrets To Unquestionable Stardom

WISDOM for DISTINCTION

Paul Enenche MD

> " The quality of your life is determined by the quality of wisdom you access and apply. "

This book presents six MAJOR principles that you should know and practice, if you must get to the place of stardom. These are the principles that have helped many rise up and stay up, and if you conscientiously go through this volume, you will never be found anymore at the bottom of life forever.

Cardinal Truth!

◈ You may boast of diverse achievements and accomplishments...

◈ You may boast of wealth and possession...

◈ You may glory in your educational qualification or attainment...

◈ You may even gloat in your strength or power – either physical or spiritual...

◈ But the truth is, everything you can glory in, is nothing compared in worth, value, and profitability to the **BLESSING OF GOD!**

INTRODUCTION ≫

So God created man in his own image, in the image of God created he him; male and female created he them. **And God blessed them**, *and God said unto them, Be fruitful, and multiply, and replenish the earth, and subdue it:...*

Genesis 1:27-28

In our world today, people boast of diverse achievements and accomplishments that they consider as assets in their lives and destinies.

Some boast of their wealth and possession. To

them, wealth is the most important asset in life. Many others glory in their educational qualification or attainment.

There are yet others who gloat in their strength or power – either physical or spiritual.

The truth, however, is that everything mortal men can glory in, is nothing compared in worth, value, and profitability to the Blessing of God.

The Blessing of God is so vital, crucial, and critical to the life and destiny of man on the earth, that it was the only thing God gave to man at creation.

With the Blessing, God knew that the future and welfare of man was secured in the earth. Genesis 1:28 says, *"And God blessed them, and God said unto them, be fruitful, and multiply, and replenish the earth, and subdue it..."*

After the flood, the Blessing was what God gave to Noah and his offspring to fulfill their purpose on the earth. Genesis 9:1 says, *"And God blessed Noah and his sons, and said unto them, be fruitful, and multiply, and replenish the earth."*

Again, when God called Abraham out of a background of failure and obscurity, it was the Blessing that was to map out his future and that of his generation.

Genesis 12:2 says, *"And I will make of thee a great nation, and I will bless, and make thy name great, and thou shall be a blessing."*

Beloved, the Blessing will do for you what no money, education, connection – what nothing under heaven can do in your life.

Get ready for a most impactful, irrecoverable, undeniable encounter with the Blessing of God in the pages that follow. You shall encounter the power, experience the products, and traverse the pathways to the Blessing of God.

Have a most blessed Adventure!

Table of Contents

Think About This!

The most important thing God gave to man at creation was *the Blessing*.

◆ All that God gave man, to begin the journey of life, was *the Blessing*.

◆ God created man and left him in the hands of *the Blessing*, as the guarantee of his future. If you are not empty of *the Blessing*, you don't have an empty future.

- *The Blessing* is far more important than money or material possessions.

- God did not give man money at creation. He gave man a spiritual materiality that cannot be calculated or quantified in human terms - *the Blessing.*

- It does not matter what anyone takes from you, if they cannot take *the Blessing*, they cannot stop your progress.

- Beloved, whatever you need to do to secure *the Blessing of God,...*

Do it!

The Blessing

PURPOSE, PRODUCTS, PATHWAYS

Experience the Substantiality, Materiality, and Tangibility of God's Blessing

AND GOD
BLESSED THEM

66

So God created man in his own image, in the image of God created he him; male and female created he them. And God blessed them, and God said unto them, Be fruitful, and multiply, and replenish the earth, and subdue it: and have dominion over the fish of the sea, and over the fowl of the air, and over every living thing that moveth upon the earth.

99

Genesis 1:27-28

Cardinal Truth!

◈ If the beginning must be well, the Blessing must be there. If the Blessing is there, the beginning is well.

◈ The most important thing God gave to man at creation was the Blessing.

◈ The Blessing is far more important than money or material possessions.

◈ If anything can get the Blessing at the beginning, that thing has succeeded well.

◈ The Blessing is a spiritual materiality, substantiality, and tangibility that is not take-able by physical or human enmity.

◈ Don't be afraid of the future if you are not without the Blessing. If you are not empty of the Blessing, you don't have an empty future

> **"**
> If your beginning must be well, the Blessing must be there. If the Blessing is there, the beginning is well.
> **"**

1

AND GOD BLESSED THEM!

ne of the most powerful forces on earth is the force of the Blessing.

But, whenever we hear the words 'bless' or 'blessing,' we don't seem to feel the 'weight' because we think that 'You are blessed' sounds more like greeting. When someone sneezes, for instance, we say, "Bless you." We have used the word until the power behind it seems to be lost.

However, there are a few things I want you to know about 'The Blessing,' that will change your life, if fully understood.

Please take note of the fact that,

THE MOST IMPORTANT THING GOD GAVE TO MAN AT CREATION WAS THE BLESSING.

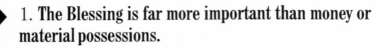

What He considered the most critical for man's survival on earth was the Blessing. The most important thing, the most valuable asset He gave to man was the blessing, and nothing more.

What that means is that:

1. The Blessing is far more important than money or material possessions.

God did not give man money at creation. He did not give him any physical or material possession. He gave him a *spiritual commodity*, *tangibility*, and *substantiality* called the **Blessing**. He gave man a *spiritual materiality* that cannot be calculated or quantified in human terms, and it is called the Blessing.

In essence, God was saying, "*I hand over to you what the world cannot hand you. I hand over to you what connections cannot hand you.*"

God was giving to man something that was beyond money, connection, education, qualification, and in fact, everything else. It is called the Blessing.

I believe that the same thing is coming upon you, in Jesus' Name.

2. God gave them the Blessing to begin their journey of life.

The Blessing is the secret of every successful new beginning. That is, if the Blessing rests on you at the beginning of anything in your life, that thing has begun well.

This is one reason why children are taken to God's altar for Blessing and dedication. That is also why houses and churches are built and dedicated, to release the Blessing upon them.

What it all means is that,

IF ANYTHING CAN GET THE BLESSING AT THE BEGINNING, THAT THING HAS SUCCEEDED WELL.

So, God was telling Adam and Eve, "*If your beginning must be well, the Blessing must be there. If the Blessing is there, the beginning is well.*"

That also means that when the Blessing arrives, something is about to begin: a new chapter or phase is about to open; a new territory is about to be conquered.

I believe that the Blessing is coming upon you for a new beginning, a new chapter, a new phase, a new opening. You are about to begin a business, career, or Ministry journey that is about to explode, in the Name of Jesus Christ.

You are too blessed to fail!

It does not matter what anyone takes from you, if they cannot take the Blessing from you, they cannot stop your beginning. They cannot stop your starting. They cannot stop your progress.

I am sure you remember the story of Joseph in Potiphar's house. Potiphar's wife took his coat, and his testimony (that he did what he did not do). She took everything from Joseph and left him naked. But what she could not take from him was the Blessing.

THE BLESSING IS A SPIRITUAL MATERIALITY, SUBSTANTIALITY, AND TANGIBILITY THAT IS NOT TAKE-ABLE BY PHYSICAL OR HUMAN ENMITY.

It does not matter how much you are hated, there is that thing that cannot be taken from you.

Why do I say this?

Joseph was accused before Potiphar, who was called *the Captain of the Guard*. When Joseph first arrived in Egypt, the Bible says that the Captain of the Guard, an officer of Pharaoh bought him. His name was Potiphar. He was the one in whose house Joseph prospered and flourished.

And Joseph was brought down to Egypt; and Potiphar, an officer of Pharaoh, captain of the guard, an Egyptian, bought him of the hands of the Ishmeelites, which had brought him down thither. And the Lord was with Joseph, and he was a prosperous man; and he was in the house of his master the Egyptian.

Genesis 39:1-2

When Potiphar's wife took Joseph's coat and falsely accused him, the Captain of the Guard was angry and threw Joseph into prison. Then he made Joseph the head of the prison.

What that means is that he made Joseph the head of high-profile prisoners like senators and governors who were in prison.

And it came to pass after these things, that the butler of the king of Egypt and his baker had offended their lord the king of Egypt. And Pharaoh was wroth against two of his officers, against the chief of the butlers, and against the chief of the bakers. And he put them in ward in the house of the captain of the guard,

into the prison, the place where Joseph was
bound. <u>And the captain of the guard charged
Joseph with them</u>, and he served them: and
they continued a season in ward.

Genesis 40:1-4

So, the Captain of the Guard gave these high-
profile prisoners to be under the control of
the same person his wife accused. In other
words, "My *wife reported you to me, but there is
something in you that makes me UNABLE to resist
you.*"

That is a paranormal situation; an
oxymoronic situation.

*I prophesy to you; may the favour that will
grant you a new beginning come upon you
now, in the Name of Jesus.*

3. **When God created man and left him in the hands of
the Blessing, He meant that the Blessing was man's
guarantee of the future.**

Beloved, don't fear for the future of the man
on whose head is the Blessing of the Lord.

God was saying to man, "*I hand over your future to the Blessing. I hand over the prospect of your life into the hands of the Blessing.*"

That is why He says in Isaiah 65:8,

> Thus saith the Lord, As the new wine is found in the cluster, and one saith, Destroy it not; for a blessing is in it:

Beloved, whatever you need to do to secure the blessing of God, do it. That Blessing guarantees your future. It makes you move like a bulldozer that has no respect for roadblocks.

Your life can't hold brakes for roadblocks because what is pushing you is heavier than what is trying to stop you. It is called the Blessing of the Lord.

Beloved, with the Blessing your future is guaranteed.

DON'T BE AFRAID OF THE FUTURE IF YOU ARE NOT WITHOUT THE BLESSING. IF YOU ARE NOT EMPTY OF THE BLESSING, YOU DON'T HAVE AN EMPTY FUTURE.

When Genesis 1:28 says, "And God *blessed them*," it meant, "And God *guaranteed their future*;" "And God *gave them a new beginning*;" "*And God gave them what money could not buy.*"

That is what is happening to you, too!

The Blessing

PURPOSE, PRODUCTS, PATHWAYS

Experience the Substantiality, Materiality, and Tangibility of God's Blessing

PURPOSE AND PRODUCTS OF THE BLESSING

And God blessed them, and God said unto them, Be fruitful, and multiply, and replenish the earth, and subdue it: and have dominion over the fish of the sea, and over the fowl of the air, and over every living thing that moveth upon the earth.

Genesis 1:28

Cardinal Truth!

◈ The Blessing has the power to bring out everything God has deposited in you.

◈ When the Blessing of God is heavy upon your life, you become multi-endowed, multiply gifted, and diversely manifested.

◈ What money cannot buy, what money can't achieve, where money is a stranger, where money is helpless, that is the realm where a Blessed man does transactions.

◈ Blessed people are strangers to indolence. They are strangers to lethargy and weakness.

◈ When the Blessing of God is upon your life, you don't beg for favour and acceptance. You don't struggle for opportunities.

◈ The Blessing makes you effortlessly in charge. You say it and see it. You have it the way you want it!

> **The Blessing makes you effortlessly in charge. You say it and see it. You have it the way you want it!**

PURPOSE AND PRODUCTS OF THE BLESSING

B eyond the foundation laid, what was the purpose of the blessing? What did the blessing come to do?

Please understand that the Blessing equals power. When God said, "Be fruitful, and multiply, and replenish the earth, and subdue it:" it was a forceful mandate. It was a mandate with the backing of supernatural force or power.

The question is, what was that power meant to achieve?

Below are seven things that the power in the Blessing came to achieve:

▶ **Power to Flourish and Blossom in the Earth.**

Power in the Blessing is 'power to flourish and blossom in the earth.'

"Be fruitful" means blossom.

God blessed them and said, "Blossom! flourish in the earth! Do not struggle or suffer to survive."

Whenever the Blessing of God is upon a life, power is upon that life to blossom and flourish.

When the Blessing of God is upon a business venture, like the business of John D. Rockefeller, the first dollar billionaire in the history of the world, that business has been empowered to flourish, succeed and blossom in the earth.

When the Blessing of God is upon a church, the witches, bitches, wizards, and lizards in the territory become too inconsequential, because there is something upon that church that is designed to make the church blossom and flourish. The children, parents, and everyone blossom and flourish.

The Blessing is the power to blossom and flourish.

Power to Compel the Cooperation and Submission of the Earth.

The Blessing is 'power to compel the cooperation and submission of the earth.'

When God blessed them, He was saying, "*I give you the power to make the earth submit.*" It is the power to compel the vegetation's submission. That is, "*By this power, the earth shall yield for you its strength.*"

You know, when Cain killed his brother, and God placed a curse on him, He said the earth shall no longer yield its strength to him. That is, the earth would not cooperate with him.

What that means is, if Cain wanted guava, the earth would bring thorns. If he wanted yam, the earth would give bad water-yam. The earth was no longer going to yield its full capacity to Cain.

> When thou tillest the ground, it shall not henceforth yield unto thee her strength;
> *-Genesis 4:12*

The Blessing is the exact opposite. It compels the cooperation and submission of the earth.

I prophesy to you:

◀ *Receive the power to receive the best of the earth!*

◀ *Receive the power to receive the best from the land where you are!*

◀ *The best of the territory where you are is released upon you!*

You are not permitted to have the worst of the land. If the Blessing of the Lord is upon your life, you are to have the choicest things and the choicest locations in the land.

Whatever is the best that the land has to offer is your portion.

3

Power to Fully Deploy In-Built Potential and Endowment

Power in the Blessing is 'power to fully deploy in-built potential and endowment.'

THE BLESSING HAS THE POWER TO BRING OUT EVERYTHING GOD HAS DEPOSITED IN YOU.

Some time ago, our music director called me to ask about the song our choir would minister during the Sunday service. I told him there was a new song already for Sunday. He checked and confirmed he actually had a song already.

Nevertheless, to avoid any confusion, I told him I would send another new song in a few minutes. Then, I received a download from ABOVE instantly and forwarded it to him. He now had options. I only advised him to choose the best.

When God blessed man He was saying, *"Receive the power to push out whatever I have put into you."* So, the Blessing makes it impossible to be impotent or have potentials that are caged or limited.

I prophesy to you:

By the Blessing of the Lord upon your life, what God has put inside you is coming out now!

Beloved, there are great things imbedded in you. It is the Blessing of the Lord that empowers you to push them out.

WHEN THE BLESSING OF GOD IS HEAVY UPON YOUR LIFE, YOU BECOME MULTI-ENDOWED, MULTIPLY GIFTED, AND DIVERSELY MANIFESTED.

When people look at you, they can say, *"That man is blessed, that woman is blessed."*

WHAT MONEY CANNOT BUY, WHAT MONEY CAN'T ACHIEVE, WHERE MONEY IS A STRANGER, WHERE MONEY IS HELPLESS, THAT IS THE REALM WHERE A BLESSED MAN DOES TRANSACTIONS.

Don't forget this for as long as you live:

- In the realm where the money man is helpless;

- In the realm where the millionaire and billionaire are stranded;

- That is the realm where the blessed man does transactions.

How did I get the song to send to our Music Director?

I just lay there and the music, melody, lyrics, and everything came complete in an instance.

It is not a 'buyable' thing. No!

Beloved get ready because something is about to come out of you!

4

Power for Diligent, Energetic and Dynamic Existence.

The power in the Blessing is power for diligent, energetic, and dynamic existence.

A blessed man or woman is a man or woman who is empowered for diligent, energetic, and dynamic existence.

Think about Abraham.

Can you remember the kind of man that Abraham was, at the age of over a hundred and twenty years?

He was still very energetic, diligent, and vibrant. After Sarah had died, Abraham married a new wife.

Is that the age to marry a new wife?

At that age, anyone would think he should be preparing to join his wife. But that was not the case with Abraham. He went ahead and married afresh. He married Keturah and had six more children.

Any old man today who is Abraham's age is already too weak for such things. He is literally on his way out. But that was the age Abraham was thinking of a new wife.

Think about Jacob

Jacob went on horseback to Egypt at the age of one hundred and thirty. How many men can do that at age 130?

Think about Isaac.

Isaac beat the whole of the Philistines until they said he was mightier than them. He lived until one hundred and eighty years.

These are the generations of the blessed.

BLESSED PEOPLE ARE STRANGERS TO INDOLENCE. THEY ARE STRANGERS TO LETHARGY AND WEAKNESS.

Some people often wonder how I am able to manage my schedule and still have the

strength to get on. Sometimes, I preach many times in one day. And I don't know for how long I preach on most occasions, daily. But the journey continues. I am 'weary-less' and 'tireless' like my Creator and Maker.

If you are a victim of weakness or sickness, I command it broken, in Jesus' Name. Whatever has brought laziness into your life, today it is arrested forever, in the Name of Jesus Christ.

5

▶ **Power to Command Favour and Acceptance**

The power in the Blessing is the power to command favour and acceptance.

That was the power God placed on Adam so that the lion, tiger, baboon, chimpanzee, hippopotamus, etc., could accept him. That is, "*Pass through their midst and be accepted and favoured.*"

Are you not surprised that Adam gave all the animals names? How did he do that? They arrived for a naming ceremony: the lion behaved itself, and the tiger could not pursue the antelope.

WHEN THE BLESSING OF GOD IS UPON YOUR LIFE, YOU DON'T BEG FOR FAVOUR AND ACCEPTANCE. YOU DON'T STRUGGLE FOR OPPORTUNITIES.

That Blessing creates a doorway for you.

And that is what is about to happen to you now!

6

► ## Power to Rule the Earth

The power in the Blessing is the power to rule the earth.

That is like saying, "*On the behalf of God, I give you the power to take charge:*

"Dominate!

"Be fruitful!

"Multiply!

"Replenish the earth!

"Subdue it!

"Take charge!

"Rule!

"I rule up, you rule down. Let us compare notes.

If anything wants to misbehave under your watch, let me know.

I extend my "rulership" to the earth through you."

That is the purpose of the Blessing.

When someone has little money, they say he is blessed. That is a tiny portion of the Blessing.

THE BLESSING MAKES YOU EFFORTLESSLY IN CHARGE. YOU SAY IT AND SEE IT. YOU HAVE IT THE WAY YOU WANT IT.

7

▶ The Blessing is Power to Fulfil Purpose

The power in the Blessing is the 'power to fulfil purpose.'

In essence, "*I place upon you this power to become everything I created you to be.*" That is the power to fulfil purpose or destiny.

So, when I pray for people to receive the Blessing, it is not just a matter of becoming happy; it is the power to fulfil purpose.

It is the power to become everything God created you to be, the devil notwithstanding, the witches and wizards notwithstanding, the hatred of people notwithstanding, the hostility of the world notwithstanding.

Beloved, it does not matter what the devil does, head or tail, you win.

It does not matter what the devil wants, by the Blessing of the Lord, you shall fulfil purpose.

◀ **What you were created for, you must become.**

◀ **What you were born to become, you must become by the Blessing, in the Name of Jesus Christ.**

I Need to Hear Your Voice Lord!

Song Received and Written
by Dr. (Pst.) Paul Enenche

Lord I need Your voice, Above all other needs
Lord I need to hear You so desperately,
For with Your voice Your Presence is assured
And with Your voice, the future is preserved

Chorus
I need to hear Your voice Lord
Above the noise of the world
Above the will of the flesh
Above every other voice

Lord I need Your voice, above all other needs
Lord I need to hear You so desperately
For with Your voice I cannot miss the way
And with Your voice, I cannot be in need

Lord I need Your voice, above all other needs
Lord I need to hear You so desperately,
For with Your voice, I connect with Your Peace
And with Your voice, my triumph is assured

The Blessing

PURPOSE, PRODUCTS, PATHWAYS

3

*Experience the Substantiality,
Materiality, and Tangibility of
God's Blessing*

PATHWAYS TO
THE BLESSING-1

66

And the Lord God commanded the man, saying,
Of every tree of the garden thou mayest freely eat:
But of the tree of the knowledge of good and evil,
thou shalt not eat of it: for in the day that thou
eatest thereof thou shalt surely die.

99

◈ **Genesis 2:16-17**

Cardinal Truth!

- Whatever connects you to the voice of God connects you to the Blessing.

- The Blessing of God travels in the vehicle of Divine direction or instructions.

- Every time there is scarcity or shortage, it is either there is something God has said that man has not heard or something man has heard and refused to act.

- The Commanded Blessing is the blessing under pressure.

- It is at your spot that your star shines. Every star has a spot. And your spot is where your star shines the brightest.

> **The Blessing of God travels in the vehicle of Divine direction or instructions.**

PATHWAYS TO THE BLESSING -1

T he foremost question on anyone's mind right now should be, what do you do to get into the river of such a loaded spiritual substantiality, materiality, and tangibility?

How do you get into that realm where you are not guessing who you are? You are aware that you are blessed! You are not assuming - you have passed the realm of assumption. You know, the devil knows, those who love you know, and even those who hate you know, that you are blessed.

How do you get there? What are the keys or pathways to the Blessing?

▶ ### Connection to the Voice of God

The Voice of God is the carrier of the Blessing of God. Within the Voice of God is the Blessing of God.

WHATEVER CONNECTS YOU TO THE VOICE OF GOD CONNECTS YOU TO THE BLESSING.

The Bible says, "*And God blessed them, and God said unto them, Be fruitful,*" (Genesis 1:28).

If you can trust God to hear Him in His Word, and hear the Voice of His direction, you can locate where His Blessing is.

The Blessing of God travels in the vehicle of Divine direction or instructions.

Deuteronomy 28:1-2 says, *"...if thou shalt hearken diligently unto the voice of the Lord thy God,... all these blessings shall come on thee, and overtake thee, if thou shalt hearken unto the voice of the Lord thy God."*

The key phrase is, "If you shall hearken!"

Learn how to go to the Lord in prayer and ask Him, *"Lord, what are you saying? What do you want from me, Lord? I don't have a choice in the matter."*

You have to come to that point where God says it, you hear it, you know it, and you walk in it.

And, even if you don't hear it audibly, you hear it from the Scripture, and run with it as if you heard it audibly.

God gave the Word to Abraham in the twelfth chapter of Genesis:

And I will make of thee a great nation, and I will bless thee, and make thy name great; and thou shalt be a blessing: And I will bless them that bless thee, and curse him that curseth thee: and in thee shall all families of the earth be blessed. Genesis 12:2-3

All these promises came in the Voice of God.

Again, in the twenty-sixth chapter of Genesis, God spoke to Isaac in the midst of a terrible famine:

> And there was a famine in the land, beside the first famine that was in the days of Abraham···And the Lord appeared unto him, and said, Go not down into Egypt; dwell in the land which I shall tell thee of: Sojourn in this land, and I will be with thee, and will bless thee;··· **Genesis 26:1-3**

The voice of God is the carrier of the Blessing of God. If only we can trust God to hear Him in His Word, and hear the voice of His direction, then we can locate where His Blessing is.

The land where our church headquarters is located on the Nigeria Federal Capital's Airport Road, was revealed by what might be described as the Voice of God or the direction of God, in a revelation of the night.

I woke up and realized that there was a place like that, with even the landmark that would show me exactly where it was.

For over twelve years, we could not locate the place, so we went ahead and bought several acres of land in other places. But the Lord said to me, "Remember where I showed you at first."

Eventually, I anointed someone to go and look for the land. I gave him landmark descriptions of the area. He went and came back with positive results.

Today, the Blessing of the Lord is speaking in that place.

Obedience to God's Instruction

It is one thing to hear the Voice of God, but another thing to obey what is heard.

You will recall that the Voice of God brought the Blessing to Adam and Eve, and disobedience to the Voice of God cut them off from the Blessing.

Genesis 2:16-17 says, "*And the Lord God commanded the man, saying, Of every tree of the garden thou mayest freely eat: But of the tree of the knowledge of good and evil, thou shalt not eat of it: for in the day that thou eatest thereof thou shalt surely die.*"

Adam and his wife rather decided to cooperate with satan the devil to disobey the Voice of God. That disobedience ushered them into irrecoverable losses and curses.

On the other hand, when God spoke to Abraham, he obeyed the Voice of God.

Genesis 12:1 says, "*Now the Lord had said unto Abram, Get thee out of thy country, and from thy kindred, and from thy father's house, unto a land that I will shew thee:*"

Abraham heard the Voice of God, obeyed, and went to the land which God spoke to him about. When he arrived there, the Blessing was already waiting for him.

In Genesis 13:2, Abraham had already exploded by obedience to God's Voice:

And Abram was very rich in cattle, in silver, and in gold.

If at any time in your life you are wondering, "Why am I not blessed," the most important question to ask God is, "Lord, is there any area of my life where I am in disobedience?"

I once said to our church some time ago, that every situation of scarcity or shortage or the lack of the Blessing is rooted in many things. But one stands out in particular: either that there is an instruction that was not heard or an instruction that was not obeyed.

It is either there is something God said but man has not heard or something He said that has not been obeyed.

You know, the widow of Zarephath said, "*I have not a cake, but an handful of meal in a barrel, and a little oil in a cruse: and, behold, I am gathering two sticks, that I may go in and dress it for me and my son, that we may eat it, and die*" (1Kings 17:12).

But God had said to the Prophet Elijah,

"*Arise, get thee to Zarephath, which belongeth to Zidon, and dwell there: behold, I have commanded a widow woman there to sustain thee*" (1Kings 17:9).

Now, because God had said, "*I have commanded a widow woman to sustain you,*" Elijah probably felt that the moment he appeared, the woman would say, "Welcome! God spoke to me about you. I have been expecting you." But the opposite was the case.

When the woman met with the Prophet Elijah, it appeared she was not aware of what Elijah was saying.

Instead of saying, "You are welcome. God has promised that everything will explode," the woman was asking, "*Who are you? What are you talking about? Are you not aware there is scarcity in this land? I am gathering two sticks to eat the last meal with my son and die.*"

In my understanding, it is either that God spoke and the woman did not hear, or that she heard and refused to believe or act.

God must have said to her, "*I am sending a prophet to you by this time tomorrow. He will come into your house. His presence will sustain you and you too will sustain him.*"

So, it is either that she did not hear Him or she heard and refused to believe or act on it, hence, she feigned ignorance.

EVERY TIME THERE IS SCARCITY OR SHORTAGE, IT IS EITHER THERE IS SOMETHING GOD HAS SAID THAT MAN HAS NOT HEARD OR SOMETHING MAN HAS HEARD AND REFUSED TO ACT.

The Psalmist said, "The Lord is my shepherd, I shall not want, he maketh me to lie down in green pastures," that is, in the midst of supplies.

The meaning of that is, "*God is the one leading me. For as long as I follow Him, I am not permitted to be in lack.*

"*If I am in lack, it is either that I am not following His direction or I am not obeying what He directed.*"

I declare...

◀ **That your ears will hear the Voice of God.**

◀ **That particular instruction that will change your life; that particular instruction that will usher you into His provision, is coming to you right now, in the Name of Jesus Christ.**

▶ ## Establishment in God's Plan

A life that is established inside God's plan is guaranteed God's Blessing. God's plan involves two things:

1. **Purpose**

2. **Place**

When we talk about God's plan, we are talking about the purpose of God for your life, and the place where that purpose should be fulfilled.

There is the place of the commanded blessing. Psalms 133:1-4 says,

> Behold, how good and how pleasant it is for brethren to dwell together in unity! It is like the precious ointment upon the head, that ran down upon the beard, even Aaron's beard: that went down to the skirts of his garments; As the dew of Hermon, and as the dew that descended upon the mountains of Zion: for <u>there the Lord commanded the blessing</u>, even life for evermore.

There is a "there" where the Blessing is waiting. 'There' is the place of the Blessing under command.

THE COMMANDED BLESSING IS THE BLESSING UNDER PRESSURE.

The Commanded Blessing is the blessing with an instruction. It is the Blessing that has been instructed to wait for a person. It is the Blessing that is under a mandate, and there is a place where such a Blessing exists.

There is a place where you are not permitted to struggle for what to eat, and not just what to eat, because what to eat is merely survival.

There is a place where you are not permitted to struggle for how to be a blessing to your generation. When you are located in that place, there is no scarcity.

When Adam disobeyed God, he was ushered out of his place of the commanded blessing - the Garden. And as long as he was ushered out of that place, he was to sweat and struggle to survive.

For Adam, where the Blessing would flourish was the Garden. And, as long as he was disconnected from that Garden by disobedience, suffering was his portion.

God told Abraham, "*If you remain in your territory, you will die in poverty. Go to the land I will show you. It is called Canaan; your blessing is in that land*" (Genesis 12:1-3, paraphrase).

Abraham stepped off into that land, and there he encountered the blessing.

Isaac was in the land of the Philistines, and God said, "*Everyone is traveling abroad into Egypt. You remain here, for 'here' is where I will bless you*" (Genesis 26:1, paraphrase).

Different strokes for different folks. We all do not have the same placement and the same purpose.

The reason why there is so much suffering in our generation is that people try to do what everyone is doing: "*Oh, everyone is getting Green Card, let me get mine, too.*"

But the truth is, Green Card does not mean green light. It may be necessary for you to have, if your purpose is connected to it.

"*Oh! Some people are migrating to Canada. They are getting residence permits in Canada!*" Someone just follows that, carries his destiny and arranges it out of sight, and out of relevance forever.

I met a man in the United Kingdom many years ago. He was a professional with a title. I wouldn't like to go into detail. He was then over sixty years old and was lamenting to me how he had been in the United Kingdom for over thirty years as a professional.

He had no pin to show that he was there.

He said he was then ashamed to go home, because he had nothing there to show, and nothing at home to show, after being trained as a professional. He most likely stepped into where God did not send him and arranged his life out of sight.

I have travelled to many countries of the world, but I do not know how much anyone can pay me to stay in America for two weeks. Such an amount does not exist, because I know where my assignment is. I am well aware of the place of my assignment.

IT IS AT YOUR SPOT THAT YOUR STAR SHINES. EVERY STAR HAS A SPOT. AND YOUR SPOT IS WHERE YOUR STAR SHINES THE BRIGHTEST.

I have had visas to over twenty countries that I could not travel till they expired. My assignment could not allow me to travel.

Some people say, "Oh, use the visa!" The question is, "Is it by force?" I do not have to travel if I don't have the time to travel.

This is where many people miss it!

A lot of people have attached themselves to jobs God did not ask them to do.

Everyone is chasing contract or property business because they're in the Federal Capital Territory. Did God tell you that property business is where your Blessing is?

"*Oh, they have called me to come and run for an elective position.*" Did God tell you your assignment is in the political arena? Must you be a politician to succeed? The most successful people in the world were not necessarily politicians.

So, we see people with the bandwagon mentality, missing their way into what God never asked them to do.

Your prayer should be, "Lord, help me to be established in your plan," and that plan equals *purpose and place.*

Purpose is, "What will I do with my life?"

Place is, "Where am I to do it?" Because you can do the right thing at the wrong place.

When Peter was asked to pay tax, Jesus sent him to the sea of Tiberias. He said, *"There is a fish there that has the answer. Open its mouth, and you'll get what you need to settle the tax collectors."*

Peter could have gone to the River Jordan with the presumption that *water is water.* And God would be saying, *"The fish waiting for you is not at the River Jordan."*

In the same vein, when God sent the Prophet Elijah to meet a widow in Zarephath, he could have gone to Bethlehem and say, "Widow is widow."

No! That's not the way it works.

God was specific. He said, "the widow of Zarephath." So, there was a particular widow in a particular location. That is the particular place where his sustenance was.

I remember when we were in medical school,

a man came to study Medicine. He was a successful Mechanical Engineer, already doing well, I think in a steel company. But he wanted to be a medical doctor at all costs. So, he came and started in the second year. He was quite advanced in age.

This man struggled and struggled in medical school. Finally, he was withdrawn in the third year, because he was unable to survive the training.

He lost his mechanical engineering job as a top person in his company. What he came to struggle for in the medical school, he could not succeed.

Do you know some parents force their children to study courses that they - the parents - could not study?

Maybe it was the ambition of a parent to be in a certain professional field, and since they couldn't, they tell their child, *"You must study Medicine. This family must have a medical doctor. This family must have a lawyer. This family must have a petrochemical engineer; we are in an oil-producing area."*

There is the story of a boy who studied Medicine and graduated successfully. During his graduation ceremony, when everyone – the community, the whole village, etc. – were gathered for his send forth party, he finished and carried his certificate to his father.

He said, *"Papa, you know you were the one who wanted to study this course. It was not in my mind at all, but I only did it to please you. This is the certificate. Please have it. As for me, I want to become a musician."*

Please tell me, Music and Medicine, are they in any way close? They may both use a theatre, but different theatres altogether.

By prophetic decree, *I declare over you:*

> **You will not miss your place.**

> **You will not miss the plan of God for your life.**

◀ *You shall be connected to the voice of God and to His Blessing.*

◀ *You will come to that place where you will never struggle for how to be a blessing to your generation.*

◀ *You will come to that point where God says it, you hear it, you know it, and you walk in it.*

◀ *Your ears will hear the particular instruction that will change your life; that particular instruction that will usher you into His provision, is coming to you right now, in the Name of Jesus Christ.*

◀ *By your encounter with the revelation in this book, God will open you up to your purpose, your place, your assignment, and His plans for your life, in Jesus' Name.*

Amen!

The Blessing

PURPOSE, PRODUCTS, PATHWAYS

4

Experience the Substantiality, Materiality, and Tangibility of God's Blessing

PATHWAYS TO
THE BLESSING-2

If they obey and serve him, they shall spend their days in prosperity, and their years in pleasures.

◆ **Job 36:11**

Cardinal Truth!

- Crookedness does not equal blessedness. Job was upright, and he was blessed.

- No matter how tempted you are, what is not licensed to you, do not take it.

- Doing the right thing may cost you initially, but it will pay you eventually.

- The Blessing that comes out of your life is a function of the blessing that flows into your life.

- When you come under the right spiritual authority, the Blessing is a natural outflow. You don't struggle for it.

- The Blessing of God is the curse-proof, trouble-proof, and struggle-proof dressing of God on a man.

> The Blessing of God is the curse-proof, trouble-proof, and struggle-proof dressing of God on a man.

PATHWAYS TO THE BLESSING -2

A re there other pathways to the blessing?

Are there other ways to access that river of loaded spiritual substantiality, materiality, and tangibility?

Of course, yes!

Walking uprightly, not Crookedly

Job 1:1 says, "*there was man in the land of Uz. This man was perfect, upright, one that feared God and reacted against evil.*"

That was the man that God so blessed in the tenth verse of Job chapter one where satan himself testified, "*have you not made a hedge about him and about his house, and about all that he has on every side, you have blessed the works of his hands and his substance is increased in the land.*"

Beloved, crookedness does not equal blessedness. This man was upright, and he was blessed.

There are so many people today, that would have even received testimony from satan about their success. That is, the devil himself would have been the one publicizing their success, but their crookedness is too much.

There are no straight deals in their life; only lying, deceit, cheating, and double deals.

Psalm 24:3 says,

Who shall ascend into the hill of the Lord? or who shall stand in his holy place? He that hath clean hands, and a pure heart; who hath not lifted up his soul unto vanity, nor sworn deceitfully.

In verse 5, he says that person shall receive the blessing from the Lord, and righteousness from the God of his salvation. This is the generation of them that seek him, that seek thy face, O Jacob. Selah.

Uprightness is very important.

It was after Adam and Eve broke the law of uprightness that they were ushered out of the Garden.

Uprightness preserved Abraham.

Abraham said to the king of Sodom, "*I will not take a shoe latchet or anything that is yours. I would not put in my hand what is not mine, in case you say you made Abraham rich."*

Those were the kind of people who were wealthy in God. They did not mix what belonged to other people with theirs.

They did not snatch people's land or dupe people. They didn't enter into a contract and renege on it or enter into deals and dupe the people at the end.

They practiced uprightness.

Listen to this: God gave Adam all things but He did not give him one thing: the fruit from the tree of the knowledge of good and evil. And the moment Adam touched that fruit, he lost the Garden.

DO YOU UNDERSTAND HOW A PERSON CAN TAKE JUST ONE FRUIT AND LOSE A WHOLE GARDEN? IS IT WORTH IT?

Some people swindled or diverted One Million Naira, and cheated someone else, and that left them stranded for the rest of their life.

Well, you can decide to eat one fruit and lose an entire garden. It's a matter of choice.

NO MATTER HOW TEMPTED YOU ARE, WHAT IS NOT LICENSED TO YOU, DO NOT TAKE IT.

Joseph said to Mrs. Potiphar, "*Your husband gave me everything but not you. Why should I do such wickedness? He gave me authority over everything in this house madam but that did not include you. Why should I do that?*" (Genesis 39:9, paraphrase).

By refusing to touch what was not his, he went into prison. But from the prison, he went to the palace.

DOING THE RIGHT THING MAY COST YOU INITIALLY, BUT IT WILL PAY YOU EVENTUALLY.

Some people may put you under pressure because you refused to give or take a bribe. They may deny you all manner of things. It may cost you initially, but it will pay you eventually.

I like you to just be patient with God. Do not struggle. Do not try to join the rat race. Do not begin to think, "*Oh! Everyone has left me behind.*" Just wait on God and follow the right path.

'Shortcut' is not really short most times. 'Shortcut' can cut short people's lives and destinies, and I have seen that many times.

Walking uprightly is a doorway to the Blessing.

That is why the things I described in previous chapters are not very common, because the people walking like that are not very many.

Living in Service to the Almighty

You shall serve the Lord your God and he shall bless your bread and your water,…

Exodus 23:25

It takes a servant's heart to connect the Blessing of God.

Do you know beloved, that God called Abraham, "My servant?" Genesis 26:24 says,

> I will bless you and will increase the number of your descendants for the sake of my servant Abraham. (NIV)

He also addressed Moses as, "My servant." Numbers 12:8 says,

> wherefore then were ye not afraid to speak against my servant Moses?

Of David, He said,

> I have found David my servant; with my holy oil have I anointed him: (Psalms 89:20)

All of them were servants.

It takes a servant's heart to connect the Blessing of God. You must be serving God, serving your generation, and servicing your generation.

Here's my counsel for you:

Do not sit in Church and do nothing.

Do not walk the streets and talk to no one.

No!

Serve God. Lead someone to Christ. Get someone saved. Contribute to someone's life in the Church.

ENSURE THAT YOUR PRESENCE IS FELT AND YOUR ABSENCE IS NOTICED.

This is because if your presence is not felt, your absence will not be noticed. And if your presence is not felt and your absence is not noticed, then your presence was not needed.

Some people are almost indisposable; I mean, they are just everywhere.

There are people that both God and man, heaven and earth, know that they are crucial, vital, and relevant to the kingdom assignment on the earth.

God keeps such people very long because His purposes are tied to their commitment.

The Bible says, '*You shall serve the Lord.*'

When I rededicated my life to Christ over three decades ago, I went to the campus fellowship at that time, entered the hall, and began to wipe the chairs and clean the place before others arrived.

That was my first time in that fellowship.

When I was done cleaning the place, I stood outside and began to usher people inside. I am sure the people who came there were wondering about the location this new usher came from.

But there was no location. It was just instant allocation.

Since that day, my zeal for Jehovah has not dropped.

There are people who do nothing for God. Nothing moves them.

Listen! You need a baptism of zeal, a baptism of passion for God that would cause the Kingdom of God to know that someone like you exists.

6

Walking in Covenant Practice

Walking in the covenant practice of giving and tithing is a pathway to the Blessing.

The first person to pay the tithe in the history of man was called Abram.

> And Melchizedek king of Salem brought forth bread and wine: and he was the priest of the most high God. And he blessed him, and said, Blessed be Abram of the most high God, possessor of heaven and earth: And blessed be the most high God, which hath delivered thine enemies into thy hand. And he gave him tithes of all. Genesis 14:18

Abram did not read about the tithe from anyone. It was not a law.

Tithing existed for almost four hundred and fifty years before the Law of Moses was given. So, it was not a matter of the Law at all. It predated the Law. It is a matter of covenant.

Paul referred to it again in Hebrews 7:7-8. He said, "*here men that die receive tithe but there he recieveth them.*"

The phrase, "He receiveth," is present continuous. That is, He is still receiving. So, the church may collect the tithe, but the person who receives it is up in heaven.

We live in a generation where people talk about things they basically have no understanding of.

Do you know one of the major reasons why Adam was pushed out of the Garden?

He ate what he was not permitted to eat.

Some time ago, after telling the story of Adam being driven out of the Garden of Eden, one of my children asked, "*Daddy who planted the Garden?*"

I said it was God.

Then she asked, "*Who planted the tree that bore the fruits of the knowledge of good and evil?*"

I said it was God.

She then asked, "*And God said they should not eat it?*"

I said, yes.

She said, "*And yet God planted it?*"

I said, yes.

She said, "*Why did He plant it if He did not want them to eat of it?*"

That was for me a tough question.

But I got to understand that God planted that tree to see whether they would obey Him voluntarily or not. God needed to know if man was obeying Him because he had no option or by his own choice.

There needed to be something to show to God that man would willingly obey or disobey if he had a choice.

So, He left man with the choice, and man failed.

Now, that is the point.

So, if God did not want man to eat of the fruit, what was he to do when the fruits from the tree dropped?

Well, he was to gather them, and at every visit God made, present them to God and say, *"This is what you said I should not eat. And since the Garden should not be dirty or untidy, I gathered them together, so I could present them to you. You know what to do with them."*

That's what he should have done.

The fruits were not meant to be eaten. They were meant to be presented to the One Who said they shouldn't be eaten. Eating that fruit cost man, the entire Garden. He had to be released.

Abraham must have gotten it by revelation through his fellowship with God: *"Do not touch ten percent of what I give you. Just send it to me."*

The tithe is a covenant connector. And for it

to be referenced again in the New Testament shows its importance.

Please find time to read my book, *Principle and Power of the Tithe*, for a deeper and clearer understanding of the tithe.

Walking Under the Right Spiritual Authority

Hebrews 7:7-8 says, "*without all contradiction, the less is blessed of the better.*"

The Bible tells us that when Abraham returned from battle, he met Melchizedek and gave him a tenth (the tithe).

Now, Melchizedek was massive enough to lay the Blessing upon Abraham, who was himself a massive blessing depot.

Also, when Jacob was brought before Pharaoh, the Bible tells us that Jacob blessed Pharaoh.

And Jacob blessed Pharaoh, and went out

from before Pharaoh. **Genesis 47:10**

Jacob knew that Pharaoh was a king, but he also knew that he himself was a prophet. And the prophet is superior to the king.

THE BLESSING THAT COMES OUT OF YOUR LIFE IS A FUNCTION OF THE BLESSING THAT FLOWS INTO YOUR LIFE.

The Blessing that is flowing out of your life is a product of the blessing flowing into your life from higher levels or quarters.

That is why you must never surrender your head to the wrong hands or surrender your ears to the wrong voice.

Adam and Eve gave their ears to the serpent. They listened to the serpent's hiss and lost everything.

This is the place of spiritual and priestly authority.

On this wise shall the priest bless the people… **Numbers 6:23**

The priest or the prophet over your life is a custodian of the Blessing of God. He is a channel and a transmitter of the Blessing of God.

Jeremiah 3:15-16 says,

> And I will give you pastors according to mine heart, which shall feed you with knowledge and understanding. And it shall come to pass, when ye be multiplied and increased in the land,···

Beloved, ensure that you are not confused about who your pastor or your prophet is. You do not choose that; God chooses for you.

Spiritual parenting is like earthly parenting. Just like you did not determine who gave birth to you in the physical, you do not determine who should be your spiritual father. God determines that for you.

He knows the content of your character and the destination of your future. He knows who has the capacity and stamina to take you where He wants you to go. He knows whose language resonates with your language.

GOD KNOWS WHO CARRIES YOUR FIRE, CAN SHARPEN FIRE WITH FIRE, AND TAKE YOU TO WHERE YOU ARE GOING.

Do not mess up with it at all, because many people are so sentimental and emotional about things, and then lose their destiny completely.

Many years ago, I listened to the message of my Father-in-the-Lord in the university, until I saw him pouring oil on my head in the dream of the night, and I pursued him.

Sometime later, he came to the town where we were, as young doctors - my wife and I.

I ran after him and I said to him, "I had a dream in the night where I saw you anointing me with oil. Can you please help me do it physically?"

He said, "Why not?"

I gave him the bottle of oil and he anointed

me with oil. I was not a pastor yet; I was still a medical doctor. But the connection and relationship started from that day. That connection has brought so many collections, and every devil can testify to it.

Beloved, make up your mind and do not let people deceive or sway you. This is not a matter of age; it is a matter of grace.

I remember a pastor who was submitting to us. Someone told him he was older than us, and should rather look for someone older to submit to. So, he disconnected himself and landed in calamity.

We respect everyone, but these are not sentimental issues. It is not a matter of age, but grace. It is not a matter of title, but mantle, and it is God who does it.

Jesus Christ who is God the Son, surrendered Himself to His own creation by name, John the Baptist, because that was the spiritual order and authority for that time.

Then cometh Jesus from Galilee to Jordan

unto John, to be baptized of him. But John forbad him, saying, I have need to be baptized of thee, and comest thou to me? And Jesus answering said unto him, Suffer it to be so now: for thus it becometh us to fulfil all righteousness. Then he suffered him.

Matthew 3:13-15

Jesus was actually saying to John, *"This is Divine order and pattern. God has put you on the scene and he has given you what it takes to announce Me to my generation, and I submit to it."*

That is the challenge of many people: Pride over nothing; arrogance where there is no need.

WHEN YOU COME UNDER THE RIGHT SPIRITUAL AUTHORITY, THE BLESSING IS A NATURAL OUTFLOW. YOU DON'T STRUGGLE FOR IT.

The blessing is the supernatural empowerment of God unto maximal and optimal existence.

It is the supernatural empowerment of God unto a profitable and successful existence.

THE BLESSING OF GOD IS THE CURSE-PROOF, TROUBLE-PROOF, AND STRUGGLE-PROOF DRESSING OF GOD ON A MAN.

It is the goodwill backing or pronouncement of God over a person's life.

The Blessing is the Divine powering or 'motorization' of human life and destiny unto success and progress.

It is the supernatural climate and atmosphere of goodness and positive results.

That Blessing is coming upon you and all that God has called you to do, in Jesus' Precious Name!

Amen!

THIS IS VERY IMPORTANT

Beloved, before you drop this book, I intend to address the most important issue, both in time and eternity. It's the matter of the soul. It's the matter of life. It's the matter of life after death.

 Please take note of the following

A. LIFE IS TERMINAL.

And as it is appointed unto men once to die, but after this the judgement: **Hebrews 9:27**

Then shall the dust return to the earth as it was: and the Spirit shall return to God who gave it. **Ecclesiastes 12:7**

B. DEATH IS NOT THE END OF LIFE.

Beyond death, life continues either in Heaven with God or in Hell with Satan.

And many of them that sleep in the dust of the earth shall awake, some to everlasting life and some to shame and everlasting contempt. **Daniel 12:2**

The wicked shall be turned into hell and all the nations that forget God. **Psalms 9:17**

And there shall in no wise enter into it anything that defileth, neither whatsoever worketh abomination, nor maketh a lie: but they which are written in the lamb's book of life. **Revelation 21:27**

C. **HOW YOU LIVE ON EARTH DETERMINES WHERE YOU WILL END IN ETERNITY.**

Let us hear the conclusion of the whole matter: Fear God and keep His Commandments: for this is the whole duty of man. For God shall bring every work into judgement, with every secret thing whether it is good or whether it is evil.
Ecclesiastes 12:13-14

So then every one of us shall give account of himself to God. **Romans 14:12**

D. WHO YOU LIVE FOR ON EARTH DETERMINES WHO YOU LIVE WITH IN ETERNITY.

Neither is there salvation in any other: for there is none other name under Heaven given among men, whereby we must be saved.
Acts 4:12

Jesus saith unto him, I am the way, the truth and the life: no man cometh to my father but by me. **John 14:6**

Beloved, in order not to end in a regrettable eternity in everlasting flames and torment, you must answer the following questions with all sincerity and accuracy:

1. Who are you living for? Who controls your life? Who directs your actions and lifestyle? Is it self, the world or Christ?

For to me to live is Christ, and to die is gain.
Philippians 1:21

2. What are the controlling desires of your life? What do you desire above every other thing in life? What drives you? Is it God, worldly pleasures or self?

> *One thing have I desired of the Lord, that will I seek after: that I may dwell in the house of the Lord all the days of my life, to behold the beauty of the Lord, and to inquire in His temple.* **Psalm 27:4**

3. What is your public testimony:

Do you represent Christ to your world?

Are you living an exemplary Christian life to the world around you?

Who do they think you are?

> *And when he had found him, he brought him unto Antioch. And it came to pass that a whole year they assembled themselves with the church, and taught much people. And the Disciples were called Christians first in Antioch.* **Acts 11:26**

> *... be thou an example of the believers, in word, in conversation, in charity, in spirit, in faith, in purity.* **1 Timothy 4:12**

4. Does God know you as His own? Is He proud of you as His Child? Can you say that He is pleased with the way you are living your life?

> Nevertheless, the foundation of God standeth sure: having this seal. The Lord knoweth them that are His. And, Let every one that nameth the name of Christ depart from iniquity. **2Timothy 2:19**

> And the Lord said unto Satan, Hast thou considered my servant Job, that there is none like him in the earth, a perfect and an upright man, one that feareth God, and eschewed evil? **Job 1:8.**

5. What are you looking forward in eternity? Are you sure that a pleasant welcome awaits you? If you had died before this time, where do you think you deserve to be, considering your actions, lifestyle and life priorities?

> For I am now ready to be offered, and the time of my departure is at hand. I have fought a good fight, I have finished my

course, I have kept the faith: Henceforth there is laid up for me a crown of righteousness, which the Lord, the righteous judge, shall give me at that day: and not to me only: but unto all them also that love his appearing. **2 Timothy 4:6-8.**

Beloved, are your answers in the affirmative to all of the above questions?

If not, it means you either need to surrender your life to the Lordship of Jesus Christ by accepting His sacrificial death on Calvary for you or you need to re-dedicate your life to Jesus Christ.

If so, pray this prayer with me:

Lord Jesus, I come before You today to surrender my life completely to you. I have lived a self-centred life that is far separated from God, I have had priorities that are not eternity-centred, I have always lived in rebellion, disobedience and sin up till now.

Lord, I am sorry for the way that I have lived

and I ask for your forgiveness and mercy. Lord, please cleanse my sins by your blood and take your place of leadership and rulership in my life.

Fill my heart Lord with the right desires and priorities. Deliver me from the vanity and fantasies of this world.

Give me the grace to say no to sin and compromise. Give me the grace to live in righteousness and represent you well in my world.

Help me to escape the tragedy of eternity in hell. Help me Lord to make heaven at the end of my journey on earth.

Help me Lord to live both in consciousness of your presence and of eternity.

Continuously reveal to me everything that would make me unworthy of Heaven.

Thank you Lord for hearing and answering me in Jesus' Name I pray, Amen.

If you have prayed this payer, please do the following:

1. Send to us your name, phone number and contact address by email: info@dunamisgospel.org or by phone: +234 803 3200 320.

2. Become serious with God by identifying with a righteousness and eternity-conscious church.

3. Study your Bible daily to receive a word from God.

4. Speak to God daily in prayer and let Him know your feelings and challenges.

5. Disconnect from every wrong association. Don't follow them to hell if they won't follow you to Heaven.

6. Speak to others about God. Share your testimony of transformed life. Be instrumental in assisting someone to escape hell.

7. Repent promptly. Do not sleep over unconfessed sins. Apply the blood over your soul for cleansing continuously. Live eternity ready.

The Lord bless you.

Contact Us

Beloved, we'd love you to share your testimonies
with us at **info@dunamisgospel.org**

OR

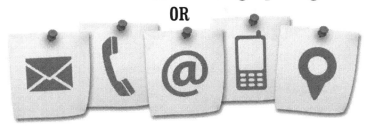

Write us a letter addressed to:

Dunamis International Gospel Centre
PMB 1677 Garki-Abuja

+234 803 3144 509; +234 807 2323 270; +234803200320

 www.dunamisgospel.org

 info@dunamisgospel.org

 drpaulenenche@dunamisgospel.org

 www.facebook/DrPastorPaulEnenche

 twitter.com/DrPaulEnenche

 www.youtube/DrPastorPaulEnenche

Worship with us @ the
GLORY DOME
Airport Road, Abuja, Nigeria

OR

Join our LIVE
services via DUNAMIS TV

Details on scanning for Dunamis TV:

1. Get a free-to-air decoder.
2. Press the MENU button
3. Enter installation (press OK)
4. Enter Pin (0000)
5. Manual Scan (press OK)
6. Scroll down to frequency menu (press the green button)
7. Enter frequency (12602) or 12600 for old receivers.
8. Symbol rate (26657) or 26630 for old receivers.
9. Polarization (vertical) if the horizontal does not change to vertical, then press the red button to change.
10. Finally, press OK for automatic scanning and wait.

WHO ARE YOU?

- What do you stand for?
- Who do you seek to please in your life?
- To succeed in your destiny and assignment, you must determine who you are.

Learn in this book how to uphold godly character in a godless world.

Learn how to live to please God daily and naturally enjoy supernatural favour.

Learn how to experience daily success triumph and fulfill your destiny against all odds.

YOU NEED GOD'S PRESERVATION IN THESE TERROR-FILLED DAYS

In times like this, when people perpetrate evil with impunity, does it mean there is no hope of security or preservation for God's people?

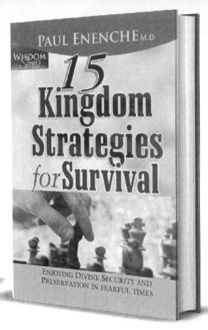

This book answers the crucial question of security or preservation for God's people and shows Divine strategies with which to access God's preservation and security in these terror-filled days.

" To live in this world without battle-consciousness is to die like chicken. To live in this world without battle-consciousness is to end as a casualty. **"**

THOU ART MY
BATTLE AXE

PAUL ENENCHE MD

This book is an eye-opener on the realm of the spirit and how we can bring the victory of our Lord Jesus Christ to our world through our individual lives.

PAPERBACK AND E-BOOK AVAILABLE

There is a Man who lived for only thirty three and a half years whose works span eternity.

This book from the stable of Dr. Paul Enenche unveils the identity of this Man and how He affects Humanity.

A

able, 23
abomination, 85
acceleration, 81
access, 48, 82, 96
accident, 7
accomplishments, 16
account, 85
accuracy, 86
address, 84, 91
advice, 80
afflict, 26
age, 79
Airport, 93
align, 78
alive, 9
all-wise, 24
AMAZON, 94
America, 30
anoint, 44
anointing, 48, 50, 70
answer, 86
Apostle, 68
appearing, 89
appoint, 26
appropriate, 78
area, 78
Arise, 33
armourbearer, 20, 50
arrive, 49, 70, 73-74
art, 10

ask, 37, 69, 78, 81, 90
asses, 43
asset, 2, 81
assignment, 8-9, 11, 29-31, 44, 77, 95
association, 46, 76, 91
assume, 29, 69
attendance, 45
attract, 30
authority, 78-79
automatic, 93
awake, 57, 85
aware, 72
Axial, 35

B

backbone, 71
baker, 21
bankrupt, 76
baptism, 78
baptize, 77, 81
battle, 97
beat, 69
beauty, 87
beggars, 71
behaviour, 79
behold, 43, 87
believe, 35, 37
belly, 4, 7
belong, 36-37
Beloved, 6, 21, 48, 84

prince, 54
principal, 58-59, 61
principalities, 20
principles, 56-58, 60-62
priorities, 88-90
prison, 11, 18, 20, 47, 52,
prize, 64-65, 68
probity, 77
produce, 9
productivity, 17, 77, 81
profession, 31
professor, 22
profit, 31, 44-46
profitable, 7, 94
programs, 73
project, 67
prominence, 2, 8-9, 19-
20, 49-50, 52, 55-56
proof, 32
property, 36
Prophet, 17, 33, 40, 42,
46, 49, 52
prophetic, 47-48, 51
prosperous, 61
proud, 88
Proverbs, 8, 14, 18
prudent, 19
Psalms, 34, 85
public, 87
pull, 44-45, 48
pulpit, 73
purity, 87

purpose, 1, 6-9, 11-12,
20-21, 23, 25, 29-30,
32, 38, 62, 74
Pursue, 12
pursuit, 5-6, 12, 69

Q

quality, 77, 80
question, 71, 96

R

Ramah, 49
random, 3, 7, 36
rate, 93
Raw, 23
reach, 65, 68, 70
Read, 94
real, 45
realization, 20, 45
realm, 36, 53, 82
rebellion, 89
recourse, 69
red, 93
release, 48
religion, 51
Repent, 91
report, 59
Republic, 30
Resonance, 35
rest, 31, 60